Federico García Lorca

Gypsy Romances

Poem of the Deep Song

English translation
Dan Veach

- STOCKCERO -

© English translation Dan Veach 2022
of this edition © Stockcero 2022

ISBN: 978-1-949938-10-4
Library of Congress Control Number: 2021953372

All rights reserved.
This book may not be reproduced, stored in a retrieval system, or transmitted, in whole or in part, in any form or by any means, electronic, mechanical, photocopying, recording, or otherwise, without written permission of Stockcero, Inc.

Set in Linotype Granjon font family typeface
Printed in the United States of America on acid-free paper.

Published by Stockcero, Inc.
3785 N.W. 82nd Avenue
Doral, FL 33166
USA
stockcero@stockcero.com

Federico García Lorca

Gypsy Romances

Poem of the Deep Song

Contents

Introduction 7

Gypsy Romances

Romance of the Moon, the Moon 19

Preciosa and the Wind 23

Quarrel..27

Sleepwalking Romance..31

The Gypsy Nun..37

The Unfaithful Wife..41

Romance of the Black Pain 45

San Miguel (Granada) 49

San Rafael (Cordova)...53

San Gabriel (Seville)..57

Arrest of Antoñito el Camborio on the Road to Seville 63

The Death of Antoñito el Camborio 67

Death from Love 71

Romance of the Summoned 75

Romance of the Spanish Civil Guard 79

Three Historical Romances 87

The Martyrdom of Saint Eulalia 87

Joke of Don Pedro on Horseback 93

Thamar and Amnon...99

Poem of The Deep Song

Little song of three rivers 107
Poem of the Gypsy *Siguiriya* 109
Poem of the *Soleá* 115
Poem of the *Saeta* 123
Portrait of the *Petenera* 129
Two Girls 135
Flamenco Vignettes... 137
Three cities 143
Six Caprices 147
Scene of the Lieutenant Colonel of the Civil Guard....151
Song of the Beaten Gypsy 155
Dialogue of Amargo 156
Song of Amargo's Mother 163
Selected Readings 165

Introduction

Federico García Lorca, one of Spain's finest poets and dramatists, was murdered in 1936 by Franco's Spanish Nationalists, who burned his books and banned their publication. Nevertheless, this unquenchable spirit would rise again after Franco's long dictatorship, to be hailed as one of the 20th century's greatest creative artists.

A multi-talented musician, artist, poet, director, actor, and dramatist, Lorca's friends regarded him with awe as a force of nature. The poet Jorge Guillén called him "an extraordinary creature…the very crossroads of Creation."

Salvador Dalí, a force of nature himself, recalled in his *Secret Life*: "The personality of Federico García Lorca produced an immense impression on me. The poetic phenomenon in its entirety and 'in the raw' presented itself before me suddenly in flesh and bone, confused, blood-red, viscous and sublime, quivering with a thousand fires of darkness and of subterranean biology…."

Federico García Lorca was born on June 5, 1898, and spent his first ten years in Fuente Vaqueros, a little farming town near Granada in southern Spain. This part of Spain is also known as Andalusia, an Arab name recalling its Moorish heritage. Here he absorbed a feeling for the Spanish countryside that was to inform all his work. The family moved to Granada, where he studied classical piano. Music, from the Impressionism of Debussy to the blood and fire of Gypsy flamenco, would be an enduring passion and inspiration.

The great turning point of his life came in 1919, when he entered the *Residencia de Estudiantes* in Madrid. In this progressive college he encountered the greatest minds of Spain, including Miguel de Unamuno, José Ortega y Gasset, and fellow Andalusian poet Juan Ramon Jiménez, who became a mentor. He would be exposed to the broader currents of Europe by Albert Einstein, H. G. Wells, Paul Valéry, Madame Curie, and Le Corbusier. And he made friends with rising artists of his own generation, like Dalí and the filmmaker Luis Buñuel.

Inspired by the music of Granada's Gypsies, Lorca began work on a book of poems about flamenco, *Poema del Cante Jondo* (*Poem of the Deep Song*), in 1921. The next year he joined with composer Manuel de Falla to host a conference on flamenco in Granada, with performances by Spain's greatest flamenco singers and guitarists.

Inspired, Lorca began work on another book, combining Gypsy themes with the form of the *romances*, Spain's popular folk ballads. At the same time he was being exposed to Surrealism through his deepening friendship with Salvador Dalí. The result was the *Romancero Gitano* (*Gypsy Romances*), a book of startling images and elusive, enigmatic stories. Appearing in 1928, it would catapult Lorca to instant fame.

This popular attention proved an embarrassment to Lorca, who only wanted an empty room, free of all social pressure, to express himself. He saw the poet as being on the side of nature rather than society. He also feared being typecast as a "Gypsy poet," dealing in primitive folklore, rather than the broadly cultured artist that he was.

Fame put a strain on his friendships too. He was already struggling with his homosexual feelings toward Dalí, who did not reciprocate them. When Dalí and Buñuel made a film called *Un Chien Andalou* (*An Andalusian Dog*), Lorca was sure they were making fun of him.

Seeing how depressed he had become, Lorca's family paid for a trip to New York in 1929. He studied at Columbia University and enjoyed spending time in Harlem, where he sympathized with the blacks, a race oppressed by the urban capitalist society which he abhorred. He found a bond between Negro spirituals and the *Cante Jondo*, the Deep Song of his native Andalusia.

He also found a model in America's Walt Whitman, whose positive, masculine homosexuality he admired. Escaping the tight confines of the *romances*, Lorca's *Poet in New York* luxuriates in spinning out long, loose, Whitmanesque lines, among them an "Ode to Walt Whitman."

These were historic times. After witnessing Wall Street's Great Crash of 1929, Lorca returned to Spain in 1930, just as her king was being overthrown and a democratic Spanish Republic established.

It was the start of a new life for Lorca. He was appointed Director of *La Barraca*, a theater troupe whose mission was to bring Spanish plays, free of charge, to rural towns and villages all over Spain. Impressed by theater's ability to speak directly to the people and advocate for social change, Lorca now turned to drama as his main focus.

"Theater," Lorca says, "is poetry that rises from the book and becomes human enough to talk and shout, weep and despair." During this time he would write and produce three now classic plays about rural Spain: *Blood Wedding, Yerma,* and *The House of Bernarda Alba*.

Blood Wedding, like the *Romancero Gitano*, was an instant success. In 1933 Lorca was invited to Buenos Aires, Argentina, to stage the play. There he also gave a famous lecture, "Theory and Play of the *Duende*," in which he said that poetic inspiration (the *duende*) depends on a vivid awareness of death, a strong connection to the nation's soil, and a realization of the limits of reason.

Conservative enemies of the Spanish Republic launched an uprising, led by General Francisco Franco, in 1936. Franco's Nationalist forces, with help from Hitler and Mussolini, took southern Spain and Granada, where Lorca was living at the time. The city's Socialist mayor, Lorca's brother-in-law, was assassinated and dragged through the streets on August 18, the same day that Lorca himself was arrested. On August 19, Lorca was taken outside the city, beaten savagely, and shot. To this day, his body has never been found.

Federico García Lorca was among the first victims of a massive purge of Spanish intellectuals carried out by Franco's regime. Lorca's books were burned in Granada's Carmen Square, and their publication was banned. It was not until the end of Franco's long dictatorship, in 1975, that it was safe to speak of Lorca's life and death.

The Gypsy *Romances*

The Spanish *romance* (often translated as "ballad") is a form of popular folk poetry that goes back to the Middle Ages. *Romance* refers not to love, but the fact that they are composed in the Spanish language, descended from *Roman* Latin. The romances, sung by wandering minstrels, included popular stories and scenes from epic poems like *The Cid*. They also served as a kind of folk "newspaper," celebrating current heroes and events.

Needing to make an immediate impact, the minstrels cut and condensed their stories, keeping only the core dramatic situation. As the tales floated free of their contexts, some acquired a mysterious, allusive quality, greatly admired by Spain's more literary poets. Learned imitations of Spain's romances were already being performed at the court of Ferdinand and Isabella. Many of Lope de Vega's classic plays took their plots and forms from the romances.

So Lorca was following a great tradition when he adapted the romance for his Gypsy poems. Its short lines were the perfect setting for his stark, surrealistic images. He wanted the sense of story that the romances provided, but also their elusive, dreamlike quality.

But if these romances are dreamlike, they are not at all vague or abstract. Lorca's images, though often baffling to the mind, are perfectly apt and precise, like the moon's "breasts of hard tin" in the very first poem. These Gypsy romances resemble one of Dalí's paintings, where things surreal —and indeed impossible— are still depicted with startling clarity.

Traditional Spanish romances are printed without verse divisions. Lorca does divide his romances into sections, indicated here by asterisks. I was amazed, however, by how perfectly most of these poems fall into verses of four lines each, reflecting the changes of subject or speaker. When it seemed appropriate, I have added "breathing spaces" where these divisions occur naturally.

THE GYPSIES

Lorca felt for Andalusia's Gypsies the way he would feel for the blacks of Harlem.

Here was a group resisting modern, materialistic civilization, a race closer to nature and real human feeling —and thus closer to music and poetry. As a poet and artist, Lorca felt like an outcast in modern society himself. He had a deep sympathy for this race that refused to modernize or assimilate, refused to give up their age-old culture, above all their music.

The Gypsies arrived in Spain around 1500 (just as the Jews and Moors were being expelled), after a long migration from northern India. The name "Gypsy" was given to them by Europeans, who mistakenly believed they came from Egypt. Their own name for themselves, the *Rom*, may be related to the Sanskrit *Dom*, meaning "low-caste people who make their living by music."

They more than lived up to that name, bringing a wild and wonderful music wherever they settled. But, fiercely loyal to their way of life, they also remained a caste apart, living on the fringes of society. In Spain, as elsewhere, the price they paid was exclusion and scorn —and an undeclared war with the Spanish Civil Guard.

The Gypsies who lived in Granada did give up their nomadic caravans —where else would you want to go, after all? Some of them settled in caves, carved out of the soft volcanic pumice hills across from the Alhambra. Although they had the world's best view, they were literal "cavemen" now, which did nothing to help their image as primitives.

But their music and dancing proved irresistibly attractive. To this day, the Gypsy caves of Granada are the place to go to hear authentic flamenco. Ironically, these cozy and perfectly insulated dwellings now command top dollar on the Granada housing market.

To celebrate authentic Gypsy music, and protect it from the taint of commercialization, Lorca and Manuel de Falla organized their Conference on the Deep Song in Granada. At the same time, Lorca was deeply immersed in his own poetic tribute to flamenco.

Poem of the Deep Song

In this book Lorca celebrates the music of the Gypsies and its place in the richly-layered culture of his native Andalusia. Flamenco's roots go back to Moorish Spain. (The intricate carvings of the Alhambra are certainly music in stone.) Into this culture, deeply infused with Oriental flavor, came the Gypsies. Their Indian music, filtered through Persia, Byzantium, and the Balkans, was strikingly exotic.

Among the forms of flamenco that have come down to us, those believed to be older and more authentically Gypsy are know as the Deep Song (*Cante Jondo*). They share a 12-beat rhythmic cycle different from anything in Western music, where 2, 3, and 4-beat patterns prevail. Lorca structures his book around four major styles of flamenco.

The most typical style of flamenco is the *Soleá*. The name is Andalusian for *soledad*, or loneliness. The Soleá lives up to its name, often dealing with heartbreak in love. Its twelve beat rhythmic cycle, or *compás*, has accents on beats 3, 6, 8, 10, and 12. Try clapping this rhythm in groups of three to hear its rather jazzy, offbeat sound:
soft soft Loud / soft soft Loud / soft Loud soft / Loud soft Loud.

The *Siguiriya* was originally sung by Gypsy blacksmiths at their forges, which figure prominently in the *Gypsy Romances*. It can be sung to the beat of a hammer on an anvil, with or without a guitar accompaniment. The deepest of Deep Songs, the Siguiriya is slow, sorrowful, and almost unbearably intense.

The *Petenera*, the story goes, began with a female flamenco singer known as *La Petenera*, so seductive that she was called "the damnation of men." Some Petenera songs decry (fondly, no doubt) her malicious charm. Lorca's poem also celebrates *La Petenera*, at whose funeral, he says, "there were no good girls."

The *Saeta* is not Gypsy in origin, though some of its songs have been strongly influenced by flamenco. Sung from the balconies during Holy Week, as statues of Jesus,

Mary, and the saints are carried through the streets below, it may justly be called the Catholic Deep Song. The name *Saeta* means "arrow," for the piercing sorrow it inspires. (Lorca puns on the two meanings frequently.) This ancient form may have Moorish and Hebrew roots as well, making it a synthesis of Andalusia's cultures.

In other sections of his *Deep Song*, Lorca pays tribute to the flamenco singers he knew, the cities that nurtured this music, the cafés where it was played, and the instruments that played it. And finally, to the spirit of the Gypsies, eternally in conflict with the staid, conservative society around them—exemplified here, as in the *Gypsy Romances*, by the Spanish Civil Guard. Thanks to Lorca, the Gypsies win this round, at least.

Gypsy Romances

"Romance of the Moon, the Moon"

Gypsies did both blacksmithing (making objects like horseshoes and knives of iron and steel) and whitesmithing, making and repairing objects of tin—whence the moon's "hard tin breasts." Gypsy blacksmiths and their forges appear frequently in these romances.

Romance of the Moon, the Moon

for Conchita García Lorca

The Moon came to the blacksmith's forge
with her bustle of spikenard flowers.
The boy is gazing, gazing.
The boy is gazing at her.

In the swirling air
the Moon sways her arms
revealing, lewd and pure
her hard tin breasts.

"Run, Moon! Run Moon, run!
If the Gypsies come
they will turn your heart
into white rings and necklaces."

"Child, let me dance.
When the Gypsies come
they will find you upon the anvil,
your little eyes closed."

"Run, Moon! Run Moon, run!
I can feel their horses now."

"Child, let me be. Do not step
upon my starched whiteness."

The horseman came closer,
beating the drum of the plains.
Inside the blacksmith's forge
the boy's eyes are closed.

* * *

Through the olive grove came
the Gypsies of bronze and of dreams.
Their heads held high,
their eyes half shut.

How the owl hooted,
oh, how she sang in the tree!
The Moon sails through the sky
holding a child by the hand.

Inside the forge they are weeping.
The Gypsies are crying aloud.
The air is watching, watching.
The air is keeping watch.

"Preciosa and the Wind"

While some of Lorca's startling images are surrealistic, others are poetic metaphors (or teasing riddles) for actual objects, like the "parchment moon" which is later revealed to be a tambourine. Saint Christopher was said to be a giant, and gigantic portraits of him are found in some Spanish churches. He was supposed to protect travelers, not menace them. The English consul may represent sober reason as opposed to the elemental passions of the Gypsies.

Preciosa and the Wind

for Dámaso Alonso

Preciosa comes playing
her parchment moon
down an amphibious pathway
of crystals and laurels.

The starless silence
fleeing from her jingle
falls where the sea beats and sings
its night full of fishes.

On the mountain peaks
the riflemen sleep
guarding white towers
where Englishmen live.

And the Gypsies of the water
amuse themselves, making
bowers of seashells
and green pine branches.

Preciosa goes playing
her moon of parchment.
The wind, which never sleeps
rouses itself when it sees her.

Giant nude Saint Christopher
full of celestial tongues
sees the girl playing
a sweet careless song.

"Child, let me lift up
your dress to see you.
Open, in my ancient fingers,
the blue rose of your belly."

* * *

Preciosa throws aside her tambourine
and runs without stopping.
The man-wind pursues her
with his burning sword.

The sea stills its murmur.
The olives turn pale.
The flutes of the shadows sing,
and the clear gong of the snow.

Run, Preciosa, run,
or the green wind will catch you!
Run, Preciosa, run!

Look, there it comes!
Satyr of low-hanging stars
with their shining tongues.

* * *

Preciosa, filled with fear
enters the house
high above the pines
where the English Consul lives.

Surprised by her cries
three guards come running,
black cloaks buckled
and caps on their heads.

The Englishman gives the Gypsy
a cup of warm milk
and a glass of gin,
which Preciosa does not drink.

While she tells them,
in tears, her adventure,
the wind, in a fury
gnaws on the slate roof tiles.

"Quarrel"

The city of Albacete was famous for its knives. Playing cards, also used to tell fortunes, may represent fate. The second four lines play upon the art of paper-cutting, then a popular way of creating profiles or cameos of people, like these "profiles of horsemen." The judge calls the dead "four Romans and five Carthaginians," harking back to the battles between Rome and Carthage in ancient Spain. He seems quite blasé about Gypsy deaths, which are merely "the usual thing."

Quarrel

for Rafael Méndez

In the midst of the valley
the knives of Albacete,
lovely with enemy blood,
gleam like fishes.

Light hard and thin as a playing card
scissors out of the bitter green
furious horses
and profiles of riders.

Into the cup of an olive tree
two old women weep.
The bull of the quarrel
is climbing the walls.

Black angels brought handkerchiefs
and water of melted snow.
Angels with enormous wings
feathered with Albacete's knives.

Juan Antonio de Montilla
rolls down the hill dead,
his body full of lilies,

his brow a pomegranate.
He now rides a cross of fire
down the highway of death.

* * *

The judge, with the Civil Guard
comes through the olive trees.
Slippery blood is howling
the mute song of the serpent.

"Good Civil Guards,
the usual thing happened here:
Four Romans fallen,
five Carthaginians dead."

* * *

The afternoon, crazy with fig trees
and murmurs of heat
falls in a faint
on the horsemen's wounded thighs.

Black angels flew
through the sunset air.
Angels with long braids
and hearts of oil.

"Sleepwalking Romance"

Granada and much of Gypsy southern Spain is located between "the ship upon the sea" and "the horse upon the mountain" of this poem's famous refrain. Green is the color of life and growth, but green flesh and skin are suggestive of death. The young and the old man envy each other's lives, but it's too late to trade risk and danger for domestic tranquility. Is the Gypsy girl alive or dead at the end of the poem? A close reading may lead to either conclusion. Or we may remain suspended, like the girl herself, over a dark pool of dreams.

Sleepwalking Romance

*for Gloria Giner
and Fernando de los Ríos*

*Green, how I want you green.
Green wind. Green branches.
The ship upon the sea
and the horse upon the mountain.*

A shadow across her waist
she sleeps on her balcony.
Green flesh, green hair
with eyes of frigid silver.

Green, how I want you green.
Under the Gypsy moon
things are looking at her
and she cannot look at them.

* * *

Green, how I want you green.
Great stars of frost
arrive with the fish of darkness
that opens the road to the dawn.

The fig tree rubs against the wind
with the sandpaper of its branches
and the mountain, a bobcat,
bristles its cactus spikes.

But who will come? From where?
Still she lies on her high balcony,
green flesh, green hair,
dreaming of the bitter sea.

"*Compadre*, I want to trade
my horse for your house
my saddle for your mirror
my knife for your blanket.
Compadre, I come bleeding
from the gates of Cabra."

"Young man, if I could
this deal would be done.
But I am no longer myself,
and my house is no longer my house."

"*Compadre*, I want to die
decently in my bed.
A steel bedstead, if possible,
with sheets of holland.
Do you not see this wound I have
from my chest to my throat?"

"Three hundred dark roses
stain your white shirt.
I smell the blood oozing
around your sash.
But I am no longer myself,
and my house is no longer my house."

"At least let me go
up to the high balcony.
Let me go! Let me go up
to the green balcony.
Balcony of the moon
where the water echoes."

* * *

The two companions go up
to the high balcony.
Leaving a track of blood.
Leaving a trail of tears.

Little tin lanterns
trembled on the eaves.
A thousand crystal tambourines
shook up the dawn.

* * *

Green, how I want you green.
Green wind. Green branches.

The two companions ascended,
the long wind leaving
a rare taste in the mouth
of bile, of mint and basil.

"*Compadre*, where is she, tell me,
where is your bitter daughter?"

"How often she waited for you!
How many times she would wait,
face fresh, hair black
on this green balcony!"

※ ※ ※

Over the face of the cistern pool
the Gypsy girl was swaying.
Green flesh, green hair
with eyes of frigid silver.
A slender icicle of moonlight
suspends her above the water.

The night turned intimate
like a little plaza.
Drunk Civil Guards
were banging at the door.

Green, how I want you green.
Green wind. Green branches.
The ship upon the sea
and the horse upon the mountain.

"The Gypsy Nun"

The title of this poem would seem like a paradox to Lorca. How could a passionate Gypsy confine herself to a monastic life? Only by pouring her dreams and passion into her art, in this case the formal, restricted confines of needlepoint.

The Gypsy Nun

for Jose Moreno Villa

Silence of mortar and myrtle.
Mallows among the fine herbs.
The nun embroiders violets
on a cloth the color of straw.

In the crystal of the chandelier
seven prismatic birds are flying.
The church in the distance grunts
like a bear, belly-up.

How well she embroiders! How gracefully!
On the straw-colored cloth
she embroiders the flowers
of her fantasy.

Such sunflowers! Magnolias made
of sequins and ribbons!
What saffron blooms, what moons
on the altar cloth!

Five grapefruits grow sweet
in the kitchen close by.
The five wounds of Christ
carved in Almería.

Through the eyes of the nun
two fine horsemen gallop.
A last deaf murmur
undoes her dress

and when she sees clouds and mountains
in the motionless distances
her heart, made of sugar
and lemon verbena, breaks.

Oh, what an elevated plain
with twenty bright suns overhead!
What rivers running at her feet
her imagination glimpses!

But she continues with her flowers
while, standing outside in the breeze,
the light continues playing chess
high above the window blinds.

"The Unfaithful Wife"

The "night of Santiago" is the festival of St. James (*San Diego or San Tiago*), the patron saint of Spain. Full of sexual images and metaphor, this is one of Lorca's most strikingly beautiful poems. With sly irony, Lorca has the Gypsy give his lover a sewing basket "the color of straw," harking back to the straw-colored needlepoint cloth of the Gypsy nun.

The Unfaithful Wife

*for Lydia Cabrera
and her little black one*

And so I took her to the river
believing that she was a maiden.
But she already had a husband.

It was the night of Santiago
and almost as if we'd arranged it.
The streetlights went out
and the crickets lit up.

On the last street corner
I touched her sleeping breasts
and they opened for me
like a bouquet of hyacinths.

The starch of her skirt
made a sound in my ear
like a piece of silk
ripped by ten knife blades.

Without silver light in their cups
the trees have grown.
A horizon of dogs
is barking, far from the river.

* * *

Passing by blackberries,
rushes and thorn trees,
under the thicket of her hair
I hollowed a bed of sand.

I took off my tie.
She took off her dress.
I, my gun belt and revolver.
She, her four undergarments.

Neither spikenards nor sea shells
have skin so fine,
nor crystals in moonlight
such glow and shine.

Her thighs sprang away
like fish surprised,
partly cold
part on fire.

That night I rode
the best of roads, mounting
a mare of mother-of-pearl
without stirrups, unbridled.

Being a man, I will not reveal
the things she said to me.
The light of understanding
has taught me courtesy.

Stained with kisses and sand
I brought her back from the river.
The swords of the iris
were swaying in the breeze.

I behaved like the man I am,
like a true-born Gypsy.
I gave her a large sewing basket
of satin the color of straw.

I did not want to fall in love
because, though she had a husband
she told me she was a maiden
when I took her to the river.

"Romance of the Black Pain"

The Spanish name *Soledad,* meaning "Solitude," comes from one of the Virgin Mary's titles, "Mary of Solitude." But it applies as well to the Gypsy flamenco form *Soleá*, whose name also means "solitude." Like the pain of the Gypsies, the *Soleá* is one of the oldest and deepest of the Deep Songs, the subject of the next book in this volume.

Romance of the Black Pain

for José Navarro Pardo

The beaks of the roosters
are digging for the dawn
when down the dark mountain
comes Soledad Montoya.

Her skin yellow copper,
smelling of horses and shadow.
Her breasts smoking anvils
moaning round songs.

"Soledad, whom are you seeking,
alone at such an hour?"

"I look for whoever I look for.
Tell me, what is it to you?
I come seeking what I seek,
my joy and my person."

"Soledad of my sorrows,
the horse that bolts and runs
will come to the ocean in the end
and be swallowed by the waves."

"Don't remind me of the sea,
for the black pain blooms
in the land of the olive tree,
beneath the murmur of its leaves."

"Soledad, what pain you bear!
What painful sorrow!
You weep tears of lemon, the taste
of waiting bitter in your mouth."

"Such great pain! I pace
my house like a madwoman,
two long braids dragging the floor
from the kitchen to the bedroom.

"Such pain! My clothes and my flesh
are turning black as jet.
Ay, for my bright embroidered dresses
and my thighs like poppies!"

"Soledad, wash your body
in water of larks
and let your heart
be at peace, Soledad Montoya."

※ ※ ※

Downhill, the river is singing,
flying with sky and with leaves.
With calabash blossoms
the new light is crowned.

Oh pain of the Gypsies!
Clean pain, and always alone.
Oh pain from a hidden spring
and a distant dawn!

"San Miguel (Granada)"

Lorca pokes gentle fun at his home town, the Church, and its saints. In its niche in the church tower, a statue of the Archangel Michael is dressed up for his feast day in "Barbary elegance" (referring to the Moorish Berbers who once ruled Granada). But all his gaudy lace and mirrors are far from nature, "far from flowers." So is the Church with its sexual repression, exemplified by the mass with separate lines for men and women. Having fun with the Church's saints for every purpose, Lorca declares Michael the saint of balloons and odd numbers.

San Miguel (Granada)

for Diego Buigas de Dalmáu

They see from the balconies
through the mountains, mountains, mountains,
mules and the shadows of mules
laden with sunflowers.

Their eyes in the shadows,
wrapped in a night immense.
In the far corners of the air
the salty dawn crackles.

A sky of white mules
closes its quicksilver eyes,
giving the quiet half-light
a farewell of hearts.

And the water turns cold
so that no one may touch it.
Water crazy, running naked
through the mountains, mountains, mountains.

San Miguel, loaded with lace
and girded about with lanterns,
shows off his beautiful thighs
in the alcove of his tower.

An archangel, domesticated,
pointing to twelve o'clock,
feigns a sweet anger
of feathers and nightingales.

San Miguel sings in the windows,
a youth of three thousand nights,
fragrant with eau-de-cologne
and far removed from flowers.

※ ※ ※

On the beach the sea dances
a poem about balconies.
The shores of the moon lose their reeds
and gain their voices.

Flashy ladies flit by
eating sunflower seeds,
butts big and occult
as planets of copper.

Tall caballeros come
and ladies of sad demeanor,
turned sepia with nostalgia
for yesterday's nightingales.

And the Bishop of Manila,
blind from saffron powder, poor,
saying the mass for two lines:
one for women, one for men.

* * *

San Miguel was quiet
in the alcove of his tower,
his gown all encrusted
with mirrors and lace.

San Miguel, king of balloons
and odd numbers,
in his Barbary elegance
of balconies and cheers.

"San Rafael (Cordova)"

Lorca depicts a town whose decay is redeemed by its fragments of classic art and architecture. Society seems to be represented by the closed-up carriages of the aristocracy, shutting out the forces of nature: the children, the fish, and the water. Like Grenada, its Archangel San Rafael is "dressed like a Moor in dark spangles."

San Rafael (Cordova)

for Juan Izquierdo Croselles

I

Closed coaches arrived
at the reed-grown banks
where waves polish
a nude Roman torso.

Coaches the Guadalquivir
spreads out on its perfect glass
between sheets of flowers
and resonance of clouds.

Children weave and sing
the disillusion of the world
close by the old coaches
lost in the nocturne.

But Cordova does not tremble
beneath the vague mystery,
for if shadow raises
a smoke architecture,
a marble foot affirms
its chaste, spare splendor.

Thin petals of tin
adorn the pure grays
of the breeze, unfurled
on the arcs of triumph.

And while the bridge sighs
ten murmurs of Neptune
tobacco sellers
flee through the broken wall.

II

One single fish in the water
unites the two Cordovas:
soft Cordova of river reeds,
Cordova of architecture.

Children with impassive faces
undress on the shore,
apprentices of Tobias
with Merlin waists,
to pester the fish
with teasing questions:
Do you prefer flowers of wine
or half-moon leaps?

But the fish, which gilds the water
and drapes the marbles in mourning,

teaches them a lesson, and the balance
of a solitary column.

The Archangel, made up
like a Moor with dark spangles
sought murmur and cradle
in the meeting of the waves.

* * *

One single fish in the water.
Two lovely Cordovas.
Cordova split by gushing streams.
Cordova dry and heavenly.

"San Gabriel (Seville)"

Seville's Archangel, unlike the other two, is a healthy force of nature, a "beautiful boy of the reeds" with a rosy complexion. The "songs of celestial mourning" he sings are no doubt the Saeta, sung during religious processions in Andalusia. (We will hear it again in the Poem of the Deep Song.) It was Gabriel who told the Virgin Mary that she was with child, a sacred event known as the Annunciation. Now, with his statue on procession through Seville, San Gabriel tells a "marvelous brown lady" (likely a Gypsy, aptly named "Anunciación") that she is also with child. But her boy, too, may have a tragic destiny.

San Gabriel (Seville)

for don Agustín Viñuales

A beautiful boy of reeds
wide shoulders, fine figure
skin of a nocturnal apple
sad mouth and big eyes
with nerves of hot silver
he roams the deserted street.

His shoes of patent leather
break through the dahlias of the air
with two rhythms that sing
brief songs of celestial mourning.

By the shores of the sea
no palm tree can equal him,
no emperor crowned
nor wandering morning star.

When he bends his head
to his jasper breast
the night looks for level ground
to bow on its knees before him.

The guitars play alone

for Archangel San Gabriel,
tamer of little doves
and enemy of willows.

San Gabriel, cries the child
in its mother's womb.
*Don't forget—the Gypsies
gave you your garments.*

II

Anunciación de los Reyes,
beloved of the moon and badly dressed,
opens her door to the splendor
coming down the street.

Archangel San Gabriel,
great-grandson of the Giralda,
between lilies and smiles
approaches to pay a visit.

Within his embroidered jacket
hidden crickets throb,
and all the night's stars
have turned into little bells.

"San Gabriel, here you have me
pierced by three nails of joy.
Your fragrance opens jasmines
upon my burning face."

"God save you, Anunciación,
you marvelous brown lady.
You will have a boy more beautiful
than the green shoots of the breeze."

"Ay, San Gabriel of my eyes!
Dear little Gabriel of my life!
To please you, I dream
of a couch of carnations."

"God save you, Anunciación,
beloved of the moon and badly dressed.
Your child will have on his chest
one mole and three wounds."

"Ay, shining San Gabriel!
Dear little Gabriel of my life!
In the depths of my breast
the warm milk springs."

"God save you, Anunciación,
mother of a hundred dynasties.
Your eyes are dry and shining
landscapes where horsemen ride."

The boy sings in her womb,
to his mother's amazement.
Three green almond bullets
tremble in his little voice.

San Gabriel now ascended
up through the air on a ladder.
The stars of the night
turned into evergreens.

Romances of Antoñito el Camborio

These two romances give two different views of a "typical" Gipsy. (We will meet another member of Lorca's fictional Camborio family in the "Romance of the Civil Guard.") In the first ballad Antoñito, a peaceful and harmless Gypsy, just can't win. Arrested by the Civil Guard for the trivial offense of picking lemons, he is reviled for putting up with such treatment peacefully, not knifing the Guards like a "real" Gypsy would. The Guards, notorious for oppressing the Gypsies, enjoy the lemonade from Camborio's lemons.

In the second romance Antoñito becomes a heroic figure, who dies defending himself valiantly (like a "real" Gypsy) against four of his cousins trying to steal his possessions. Ironically, he asks his literary creator, "Federico García" (Lorca himself), to call the Civil Guard. But it seems the cousins will get away with murder: to the Civil Guards, killing a Gypsy is less of a crime than picking lemons. Between these two romances we may see the tragedy of an oppressed race, quarreling violently among themselves rather than attacking their true oppressor.

ARREST OF ANTOÑITO EL CAMBORIO ON THE ROAD TO SEVILLE

for Margarita Xirgu

Antonio Torres Heredia
son and grandson of Camborios
with a willow staff is walking
to Seville to see the bullfights.

Brown man of the green moon,
he travels slowly and graciously.
The blued-steel ringlets of his hair
shine between his eyes.

Halfway along the road
he cut some round lemons
and was throwing them into the water
until it turned to gold.

And halfway along the road
beneath the branches of an elm
the highway Civil Guard
took him by the elbows.

* * *

The day goes by slowly,
the afternoon slung on a shoulder
like a bullfighter's jacket
over the sea and the canyons.

The olive trees await
the night of Capricorn
and a brief equestrian breeze
leaps over the mountains of lead.

Antonio Torres Heredia
son and grandson of Camborios
is walking without his willow staff
between five tri-cornered hats.

"Antonio, who are you?
If you call yourself a Camborio,
you would have made by now
a fountain of blood with five spouts.
No, you are no one's son,
no true-born Camborio."

No more are those Gypsies
who roamed the mountains alone!
The ancient knives
are shivering in the dust.

*＊＊

At nine at night
they take him to the calaboose
while all the Civil Guards
drink lemonade.

At nine at night
they shut him in the calaboose
while the sky is shining
like a horse's ass.

The Death of Antoñito el Camborio

for José Antonio Rubio Sacristán

Voices of death were keening
close by the Guadalquivir.
Ancient voices surrounding
the voice of manhood's flower.

He gored their wineskins
with a wild boar's bites.
In the fight he leapt
clean as a dolphin.

He bathed his cravat
in the blood of his foes,
but they were four knives
and he had to fall.

When the stars stab
the gray water with their daggers,
when young oxen dream
Veronicas of violets,
voices of death are keening
close by the Guadalquivir.

* * *

"Antonio Torres Heredia,
Camborio tough as horsehair,
brown man of the green moon,
the voice of manhood's flower:
Who has taken your life
close by the Guadalquivir?"

"My four Heredia cousins,
the sons of Benameji.
What they did not envy in others,
they envied in me:

"Shoes the color of oxblood
medallions of ivory
and this skin of mine, kneaded
with olive oil and jasmine."

"Ay, Antoñito el Camborio,
worthy of any empress!
Remember the Virgin now,
because you are going to die."

"Ay, Federico García,
call the Civil Guard!
My body is broken
like a stalk of corn."

* * *

He had three bloody wounds
and he died in profile,
a living coin
that will never be struck again.

A faded angel placed
his head upon a cushion.
Others, with a tired blush
lit candles.

By the time the four cousins
reached Benamejí
the voices of death ceased their keening
close by the Guadalquivir.

"Muerto de Amor"

"Those people" smelting copper are, of course, the Gypsy blacksmiths. "Facades of lime" refers to the quicklime used to whitewash houses.

Death from Love

for Margarita Manso

What is that shining
through the high streets?

"Close the door, my son.
It has just struck eleven."

"In my eyes, unbidden
four lanterns are glowing."

"It must be those people
are forging copper."

              * * *

Garlic of anguished silver,
the waning moon
adorns with yellow tresses
the yellow towers.

The trembling night knocks
at the crystal balconies,
persecuted by a thousand dogs
that do not know her.

A scent of wine and incense
drifts down the streets.

* * *

Breezes from wet reeds
and whispers of ancient voices
resound through the broken arch
of midnight.

Oxen and roses were sleeping,
but through the streets
the four lights were crying
with the fury of St. George.

Sad ladies of the valley
laid down the blood of their men,
tranquil as cut flowers
bitter as young thighs.

Old women of the river
wept at the foot of the mountain
an endless minute
of flowing hair and names.

Facades of lime
made the night white and square.
Seraphim and Gypsies
were playing accordions.

"Mother, when I die
let people know about it.
Send blue telegrams
from South to North."

Seven cries, seven bloods
seven opium poppies
broke opaque moons
in darkened rooms.

Full of severed hands
and little crowns of flowers
the sea of curses thundered
I don't know where.

And the sky slammed its doors
on the rude noise from the woods
while on the high streets
the lights were screaming.

"Romance of the Summoned"

This is one of the most eerie and vivid descriptions of dying in all of literature. The "icy cards" would be fortune-teller's cards, like the Tarot. "The dense oxen of the water" is one of Lorca's most admired lines. Amargo, whose name means "bitter," made his first appearance in *Poem of the Deep Song*. For more about him, see the notes to that book below.

Romance of the Summoned

for Emilio Aladrén

My solitude without rest!
The small eyes of my body
and the big eyes of my horse
never close at night
nor look to the other side
where a dream of thirteen ships
is peacefully sailing away.

Instead, hard and clean,
vigilant squires, my eyes
stare at a north
of metals and mountain crags
where my veinless body
consults the icy cards.

* * *

The dense oxen of the water
are bumping against the boys
who bathe in the moons
of their undulant horns.

And the hammers sang
on the sleepwalking anvils
the insomnia of the rider
the insomnia of the horse.

* * *

The twenty-fifth of June
they said to Amargo:
"Now you can cut, if you wish,
the oleanders on your patio.
Put a cross on your door
and put your name beneath it,
because hemlocks and nettles
will grow in your guts
and needles of wet lime
gnaw on your shoes.

"It will be night, in the dark
of the magnetized mountains
where the oxen of water
are drinking the rushes, dreaming.

"Ask for lights and for bells.
Learn to cross your hands
and enjoy the cold winds
of metals and mountain crags.
Because two months from today
you will be stretched out in a shroud."

* * *

St. James waves through the air
his broadsword of fog.
Grave, silent, behind his back
the warped sky arose.

* * *

The twenty-fifth of June
Amargo opened his eyes
and the twenty-fifth of August
he lay down to close them.

Men came down the street
to see the one summoned,
who stared at the wall,
his solitude now at rest.

The impeccable sheet
with its stern Roman speech
gave composure to his death
with its straight, square cloth.

"Romance of the Spanish Civil Guard"

One of Lorca's greatest poems, and a fitting end to the Gypsy romances in this book: a final, cataclysmic confrontation between the Gypsies and their ancient enemy. The city is Jerez de la Frontera, an Andalusian town famous for its sherry wine ("sherry" is an English attempt to say "Jerez.") The Virgin and Saint Joseph appear in the guise of statues paraded in religious processions, whence their gaudy dress. Because this is Jerez, Pedro Domecq, a famous maker of sherry, also joins the parade.

As the Guard attacks, it is clear which side true Christianity is on: the Virgin and Saint Joseph, wounded himself, try to help and protect the Gypsies. A Gypsy woman, Rosa of the Camborios, is martyred like Saint Eulalia (whose story is told in the following poem). Among the unforgettable images of this poem, one wonders if Picasso adopted Lorca's wounded horse as the central figure for his painting *Guernica*.

Romance of the Spanish Civil Guard

*for Juan Guerrero,
Consul General of poetry*

Their horses are black.
Their horseshoes are black.
Upon their capes are shining
stains of ink and sealing wax.

Skulls made of lead,
they never cry.
With souls of patent leather
they ride down the highway.

Hunchbacked, nocturnal
imposing, wherever they go
dark rubber silences
fine sands of fear.

They go wherever they wish,
hiding within their heads
a vague astronomy
of impalpable pistols.

* * *

Oh city of the Gypsies!
Street corners with flags and banners.
The moon and the pumpkin
with cherry conserves.

Oh city of the Gypsies!
Who has seen you and does not remember?
City of sorrows and musk.
City of cinnamon towers.

* * *

When the night came,
night of all nocturnal nights,
the Gypsies were at their forges
forging suns and arrows.

A mortally wounded horse
was crying at every door.
Roosters of glass were singing
in Jerez de la Frontera.

The naked wind turns
the corner of surprise
in the platinum night,
night of all nocturnal nights.

* * *

The Virgin and Saint Joseph
have lost their castanets
and seek out the Gypsies
to see if they can find them.

The Virgin comes dressed
like a mayor's wife,
wrapped in chocolate foil
and necklaces of almonds.

Saint Joseph is swinging his arms
under a cape of silk.
Behind him comes Pedro Domecq
and three sultans of Persia.

The half moon is dreaming
an ecstasy of storks.
Banners and lanterns
take over the roofs.

Sobbing in the mirrors
were dancers without hips.
Water and shadow, shadow and water
in Jerez de la Frontera.

* * *

Oh city of the Gypsies!
Street corners with flags and banners.
Extinguish your green glowing lights—
the Civil Guard is coming.

Oh city of the Gypsies!
Who has seen you and does not remember?
Leave her far from the sea,
without any combs for her tresses.

* * *

They advance two by two
on the festival city.
The rustle of dry onion skin
invades their cartridge pouches.

They advance two by two.
Double night of dark cloth.
For them, the sky
is a showcase for their spurs.

* * *

The city, fearless
multiplied its gates.
Forty Civil Guards
enter, intent upon plunder.

The clocks all stopped
and the cognac in the bottles
disguised itself as November
so as not to arouse suspicion.

A flight of long screams
arose from the weathercocks.
Sabers slash the breezes
that horse hooves trample.

Down shadowy streets
old Gypsy women are fleeing
with half-asleep horses
and coins in cookie jars.

Up the steep streets
come the sinister capes.
In their wake, fleeting
whirlwinds of scissors.

* * *

At the stable of Bethlehem
the Gypsies gather.
Saint Joseph, covered with wounds,
shrouds the corpse of a maiden.

Stubborn, sharp rifle shots
resound through the night.
The Virgin heals children
with spittle from a star.

But the Civil Guard
advances, igniting bonfires
where, young and naked
the imagination burns.

Rosa of the Camborios
groans at her gate,
her two breasts cut off
and placed on a tray.

The other girls ran
pursued by their braided hair
through air exploding
with roses of black gunpowder.

When all the tile rooftops
furrowed the earth
the dawn shook its shoulders
vast profile of stone.

* * *

Oh city of the Gypsies!
The Civil Guard disappears
down a tunnel of silence
while the flames surround you.

Oh city of the Gypsies!
Who has seen you and does not remember?
Let them look for you in my forehead.
Play of the moon and the sand.

Three Historical Romances

These final three poems do not deal with Gypsies, and might well have been placed in another book. "Eulalia" and "Thamar" are spectacular examples of Lorca at the height of his powers, however, and not to be missed. "Don Pedro," on the other hand, could just as well be dropped into the nearest *laguna*.

"Martyrdom of Saint Eulalia"

This is a shockingly vivid portrayal of the martyrdom of a young Spanish Christian girl, which took place in Merida, a city built by the Romans, in 304 A.D. Eulalia (*Santa Olalla*) was Spain's most important saint until the rise of the cult of Saint James at Compostela. Lorca's depiction varies somewhat from the usual accounts of her martyrdom, which themselves involve a good deal of imagination.

Three Historical Romances
The Martyrdom of Saint Eulalia

for Rafael Martínez Nadal

I. Panorama of Mérida

Down the street prances and gallops
a long-tailed horse,
while old Roman soldiers
cast lots or sleep.

In its midst, Minerva's mountain
opens its leafless arms.
Spray surrounds
the edges of its cliffs.

Night of prostrate torsos
and broken-nosed stars
awaiting the cracks of dawn
to crumble completely.

Red-crested blasphemies
sounded from time to time.
When the holy girl moans
she shatters the crystal glasses.

The grindstone whets knives
and scythes with sharp hooks.

The bull of the anvil bellows
and Mérida crowns herself
with sleepy spikenards
and blackberry brambles.

II. The Martyrdom

Nude Flora ascends
on stairways of water.
The Consul asks for a tray
for Eulalia's breasts.

A flush of green veins
breaks out on her neck.
Her sex trembles, caught
like a bird in the brambles.

On the ground, spasmodic,
her severed hands flounder,
still able to cross themselves
in a delicate, decapitated prayer.

Through the red mouths
where her breasts had been
small heavens are seen,
and streams of white milk.

A thousand tiny trees of blood
completely cover her back,
opposing wet trunks
to the scalpel of flames.

Yellow centurions
with gray flesh, awakened
arrive in heaven
clashing their silver armor.

Meanwhile, in trembling confusion
a passion of horsehair and swords
the Consul carries on a tray
Saint Eulalia's smoking breasts.

III. Inferno and Glory

Rippled snow rests.
Eulalia is hanging from the tree.
Her charcoal nakedness
blackens the icy breeze.

The tense night gleams.
Eulalia dead on the tree.
The inkwells of the cities
slowly spill their ink.

Black tailor's mannequins
cover the snow of the fields
in long lines that groan
their mutilated silence.

Fine snow begins.
Eulalia white on the tree.
Squadrons of silvery nickel
stick beaks in her side.

* * *

A reliquary of the Host
shines on the burned-out skies
between canyon throats
and nightingales in branches.

Stained glass dances!
Eulalia white on white.
Angels and Seraphim
chanting *Holy, Holy, Holy*.

"Joke of Don Pedro on Horseback"

Coming after the horrifying scenes of "Eulalia," this seems a rather weak attempt at humor, making a pun on *lagunas*, which can mean either "lakes" or interruptions in the verse.

Joke of Don Pedro on Horseback

Ballad with *lagunas*

for Jean Cassou

Down the path
came Don Pedro.
Ay, how he cried
that caballero!

Upon an agile horse
without a bridle
he came looking
for bread and kisses.

All the windows
are asking the wind
about the obscure crying
of the caballero.

First *Laguna*

Under the water
the words go on.

Upon the water
a round moon
is bathing,
making the other one
envious—up so high!
On the bank
a child sees the moon
and says
"Night, play your cymbals!"

Going on

Don Pedro arrives
at a distant city.
A city of gold
in a forest of cedars.
Is it Bethlehem? In the air
rosemary and lemon verbena.
The roof tiles and clouds
are shining. Don Pedro
passes through broken arches.
Two women and one old man
come out to meet him
with silver lamps.
The poplar trees say "No."
The nightingale says "We shall see."

Second *Laguna*

Under the water
the words go on.
Upon the water's tresses
a circle of flames and birds.
Among the reeds
witnesses who know what is missing.
Sleep of guitar wood
solid, with no north star.

Going on

Along the level road
two women and one old man
go to the cemetery
with silver lamps.
Among the saffron flowers
they have discovered, dead
the somber horse
of Don Pedro.
The secret voice of afternoon
was bleating in the sky.
The unicorn of absence
shatters his horn like glass.
The grand, distant city
is burning
and a man goes weeping
in that land.
To the North, a star.
To the South, a sailor.

Last *Laguna*

Under the water
are words.
The muck of lost voices.
Upon the cold surface
Don Pedro—forgotten, alas,
is playing with the frogs.

"Thamar and Amnon"

From the Biblical story of King David's son Amnon, who raped his half-sister Thamar (2nd Samuel, chapter 13). Seldom has the onset of sexual desire been depicted more convincingly, in imagery seductive as the *Song of Songs*.

Thamar and Amnon

for Alfonso García-Valdecasas

The moon circles the sky
high over waterless lands
while summer sows rumors
of flames and tigers.

Nerves of metal
resounded on the roofs.
Curling air came
with the bleating of wool.

The land offers itself
full of wounds and scars,
shudders with white light's
sharp, burning cautery.

※ ※ ※

Thamar was sleeping,
birds in her throat,
to the sound of icy tambourines
and moonstruck zithers.

Her nakedness under the eaves
due north of the palm

begs for snowflakes on her belly,
sleet upon her shoulders.

Thamar was singing
naked on her terrace.
Around her feet,
five frigid doves.

Amnon, slim and solid,
saw her from the tower.
His loins filled with sea foam
his beard with trembling.

Her sunlit nakedness
was stretched out on the terrace
with a whisper between her teeth
of an arrow that just struck home.

Amnon was watching
the moon, round and low
and saw there the very firm
breasts of his sister.

* * *

Amnon, at half past three
lay down on his bed.
The whole bedroom ached
with his eyes full of wings.

The ripening light
hides towns in brown sand,
uncovers a fleeting coral
of dahlias and roses.

Lymph from a pent-up well
spills its silence into the jars.
In the moss of tree limbs
the uncoiled cobra sings.

Amnon groans
on the bed's cool sheets.
Ivy of chills and fever
creeps over his burning flesh.

Thamar entered the quiet
of the bedroom silently,
the color of veins and the Danube
disturbed by distant signs.

"Thamar, extinguish my eyes
within your eternal dawn.
The threads of my blood
are weaving veils around your dress."

"Brother, leave me in peace.
Your kisses upon my back
are wasps and little breezes
in a double swarm of flutes."

"Thamar, in your upright breasts
two fish are calling out to me
and in the buds of your fingertips
the rumor of a rose within."

* * *

The hundred horses of the king
are whinnying in the courtyard.
Sun in cubes weighed down
upon the slender vines.

Now he grabs her by the hair
now he is ripping her dress.
Warm corals are drawing
rivulets on a red map.

* * *

Oh, what cries were heard
on the rooftops!
What a flurry of daggers
and tunics torn.

On the sad stairways
slaves climb and descend.
Pistons and thighs are playing
under the clouds, stopped and still.

All around Thamar
virgin Gypsies are screaming

while others collect the drops
from her martyred flower.

White cloth turns red
behind closed bedroom doors.
Warm whispers of dawn
exchange tendrils and fishes.

* * *

The furious rapist
Amnon escapes on his horse.
Blacks shoot arrows after him
from walls and watchtowers.

When the four hooves
were four distant echoes
King David took scissors
and cut his harp strings.

Poem of the Deep Song

For a description of the various flamenco forms celebrated in this book, please see the Introduction. To enjoy these marvelously impressionistic poems, the best advice is *abandon yourself to the music*!

At the end of this book, after all the flamenco poems, are two theatrical scenes and two poems that will herald the birth of Lorca's *Gypsy Romances*. The first is a conversation between an arrogant lieutenant of the Civil Guard and a Gypsy, whose deeply poetic responses make the Civil Guard apoplectic. The following "Song of the Beaten Gypsy" could be called Lorca's first Gypsy romance.

The next theatrical scene features the Gypsy Amargo, whose name means "bitter," as its central figure. Lorca tells how he first met Amargo:

> "When I was eight years old, playing in my house in Fuente Vaqueros, there appeared at the window a boy who looked like a giant. He stared at me with a scorn and hatred I will never forget, and spit into the house before he left. In the distance I heard a voice calling, 'Amargo, come!'" (Stockcero 145)

Lorca became obsessed with understanding this "angel of death and desperation," so emblematic of his native Andalusia and her Gypsies. In the "Dialog," Amargo becomes a sympathetic character, who tries to refuse the knife the strange horseman offers. In the final poem, his mother refers to her pain as "the cross," but vows to go on without crying. The final line presages the first of the *Gypsy Romances:* "Amargo is there on the moon."

Poem of The Deep Song

Little song of three rivers

for Salvador Quintero

The river Guadalquivir
runs between oranges and olives.
The two rivers of Granada
descend from the snow to the wheat.

*Oh love
that left and never returned!*

The river Guadalquivir
has garnet whiskers.
The two rivers of Granada
one of tears, the other blood.

*Oh love
that flew away on the wind!*

Seville has a road
for sailing ships.
On Granada's streams
only sighs row the waters.

*Oh love
that left and never returned!*

Guadalquivir, a high tower
and wind in the orange groves.
Dauro, Genil, little turrets
dead above stagnant ponds.

Oh love
that flew away on the wind!

Some say that the water carries
a ghost light of screams.

Oh love
that left and never returned!

But it bears citrus flowers and olives
Andalusia, to your seas.

Oh love
that flew away on the wind!

Poem of the Gypsy *Siguiriya*

for Carlos Morla Vicuña

Landscape

The field
of olives
opens and closes
like a fan.
Above the olive grove
is a sunken sky
and a dark rain
of cold stars.
Rushes and twilight tremble
on the riverbank.
The gray air curls up.
The olives
are heavy
with cries.
A covey
of captive birds
waving their long
tails in the shade.

The guitar

The guitar
begins to weep.
The wineglasses of dawn
are shattered.
The guitar
begins to weep.
It is useless to silence it.
It is impossible
to silence it.
Monotonous lament
like the weeping of water,
like the wind weeps
over the snow.
It is impossible to silence it,
weeping for things far away.
Sand of the hot South
asking for white camellias.
Cry of an arrow without a target
afternoon without morning
and the first dead bird
on the branch.
Oh guitar!
Heart fatally wounded
by five swords.

The cry

The ellipse of a cry
goes from mountain
to mountain.

Out of the olive trees,
a black rainbow
on the blue night.

Ay!

Like a viola's bow
the cry vibrates
the long strings of the wind.

Ay!

(The people of the caves
bring out their lamps.)

Ay!

The Silence

Listen, my child, to the silence.
It's an undulating silence,
a silence
where valleys and echoes slip
and faces turn
toward the ground.

The *Siguiriya* passes by

Among the black butterflies
a brown girl walks
along with a white snake
of fog.

Land of light
sky of earth.

Chained to a rumble
of rhythm that never arrives,
her heart is silver.
Her right hand holds a knife.

Where are you going, *siguiriya*,
with your decapitated rhythm?
What moon will gather
your sadness of whitewash and oleander?

Land of light
sky of earth.

After passing

The children gaze
at a faraway place.

Candles snuff themselves out.
Blind girls
question the moon
and spirals of wailing
ascend through the air.

The mountains gaze
at a faraway place.

And after that

The labyrinths
that time created
disappear.

(All that is left
is the desert.)

The heart,
fount of desire,
disappears.

(All that is left
is the desert.)

The illusion of dawn
and kisses
disappear.

All that is left
is the desert,
the undulating
desert.

Poem of the *Soleá*

for Jorge Zalamea

Dry Land

Dry land,
quiet land
of nights
immense.

Wind in the olive grove,
wind in the mountains.

Ancient
land
of lamps
and suffering.
Land
of deep cisterns.
Land
of death without eyes
and arrows.

Wind on the roads.
Breeze in the poplar trees.

Town

Upon the bald hill
a Calvary.
Clear water,
olives centuries old.
In the narrow lanes
men in cloaks,
and on the towers
weathercocks turning.
Eternally
turning.
Oh, lost little town
in the Andalusia of weeping!

Dagger

The dagger
enters the heart
like the blade of a plow
enters virgin soil.

No.
Don't stab me with it.
No.

The dagger
like a ray of sunlight
illumines
the terrible depths.

No.
Don't stab me with it.
No.

Crossroads

Wind from the East,
a lantern
and a dagger
in the heart.
The street
is vibrating
like a string
pulled tight,
buzzing
like an enormous hornet.
On every side
I
see the dagger
in the heart.

Ay!

In the wind, the cry leaves
the shadow of a cypress.

(Leave me here in this field,
weeping.)

Everything has broken in the world.
Nothing remains but silence.

(Leave me here in this field,
weeping.)

The horizon without light
is bitten by bonfires.

(I've told you to leave me
here in this field
weeping.)

Surprise

Dead in the street
with a knife in his chest.
Nobody knew him.
How the streetlight trembled!
Mother.

How the little streetlight
trembled!
It was dawn. Nobody
could bear to look at his eyes,
open to the hard air.
He lay there, dead in the street
with a knife in his chest
and nobody knew him, nobody.

The *Soleá*

Dressed in black mantillas,
she thinks the world is small
and the heart immense.

Dressed in black mantillas.

She thinks the tender sigh
and the cry both disappear
in the current of the wind.

Dressed in black mantillas.

She left her balcony open
and at dawn the whole sky
flooded in through her balcony.

*Ay yayayayay,
dressed in black mantillas!*

Cave

Out of the cave
come long sobs.

(The purple
upon the red.)

The Gypsy evokes
distant lands.

(High towers,
mysterious men.)

His eyes
follow his broken voice.

(The black
upon the red.)

And the whitewashed cave
trembles in the gold.

(The white
upon the red.)

Encounter

Neither you nor I
are in any condition
to meet one another.
You… you know why.
I loved her so much!
Follow this little path.
In my hands
I have holes
from the nails.
Don't you see how
I'm bleeding to death?
Never look back,
go slow
and pray as I do
to San Cayetano,
for neither you nor I
are in any condition
to meet one another.

Dawn

Bells of Cordova
in the morning.
Bells of dawn
in Granada.
All the girls hear you
singing the tender,
mourning *soleá*.
The girls
from high and low
Andalusia.
The girls of Spain
with small feet
and quivering skirts
who fill up the crossroads
with lights.
Oh bells of Cordova
in the morning.
And oh, bells of dawn
in Granada!

Poem of the *Saeta*

for Francisco Iglesias

Archers

The dark archers
are approaching Seville.

The Guadalquivir is open.

Broad gray sombreros,
long heavy capes.

Ay, Guadalquivir!

They come from the distant
nations of pain.

The Guadalquivir is open.

They enter a labyrinth.
Love, crystal, and stone.

Ay, Guadalquivir!

Night

Candle, oil lamp
lantern and firefly.

The constellation
of the saeta.

Little golden windows
tremble,
crosses begin to stir
and superimpose themselves
upon the dawn.

Candle, oil lamp
lantern and firefly.

Seville

Seville is a tower
full of fine archers.

Seville to wound.
Cordova to die.

A city that lies in wait
for long rhythms

and twists them
like labyrinths.
Like the stems
of grapevines on fire.

Seville to wound!

Under the arc of sky
upon her clean plain
she utters the incessant
saeta of her river.

Cordova to die!

And crazed with her horizon
she mixes into her wine
Don Juan's bitterness,
the perfection of Dionysus.

Seville to wound.
Always Seville to wound!

Procession

Strange unicorns
come down the street.
From what field,
what mythical forest?

Closer up
they look like astronomers.
Fantastic Merlins
and the *Ecce Homo*
enchanted Durandarte
Orlando Furioso.

Icon

Virgin in a hoop skirt,
Virgin of Solitude,
open as an enormous
tulip.
In your ship of lights
you sail
on the high tide
of the city, in between
the turbulence of saetas
and crystal stars.
Virgin in a hoop skirt,
you sail
the river of the street
down to the sea!

SAETA

A brown Christ
changes
from the lily of Judea
to the carnation of Spain.

Look at him, where he is coming from!

From Spain.
Sky clean and dark,
parched earth,
streams where the water
runs slow.
Brown Christ
with burned-black locks
high cheekbones
and pupils white.

Look at him, where he is going!

BALCONY

La Lola
sings *saetas*.
The young bullfighters
surround her
and the little barber
from his doorway
nods her rhythms
with his head.

Amid the sweet basil
and the peppermint
La Lola sings
saetas.
La Lola, the one
who gazed for so long
at her reflection in the pool.

Daybreak

But like love,
those who sing the *saeta*
are blind.

In the green night
their arrows
leave a trail
of burning lilies.

The keel of the moon
breaks through violet clouds.
Their quivers
fill up with dew.

Ay, but like love
those who sing the *saeta*
are blind!

Portrait of the *Petenera*

for Eugenio Montes

Bell

(Bass String)

In the yellow tower
tolls a bell.

On the yellow wind
the bell tones bloom.

In the yellow tower
the bell stops ringing.

The wind in the dust
is a ship's silver prow.

The Road

One hundred horsemen
dressed in mourning.
Where will they go
through the orange grove's
stretched-out sky?

Not to Cordova or Seville
will they come.
Nor to Granada that sighs
for the sea.
These dreaming horses
will carry them
to the labyrinth of crosses
where the song is trembling.
Pierced by seven *ays!*
where will they go,
the hundred Andalusian horsemen
of the orange grove?

The six strings

The guitar
makes dreams cry.
The sobbing
of lost souls
escapes its
round mouth.
And like the tarantula
spins a great star
to trap the sighs
which float in its black
pool of wood.

Dance
In the Garden of La Petenera

In the night of the garden
six Gypsies
dressed in white
are dancing.

In the night of the garden
crowned
with jasmine
and paper roses

In the night of the garden
their teeth,
mother-of-pearl,
inscribe the burnt dark.

In the night of the garden
their violet shadows
lengthen
into the sky.

Death of *La Petenera*

In the white house lies dying
the damnation of men.

A hundred horses are prancing.

Their riders are dead.

Under the lamps'
shaking stars
her silk skirt is trembling
between her copper thighs.

A hundred horses are prancing.
Their riders are dead.

Long, sharp-edged shadows
stretch from the troubled horizon.
The bass string of the guitar
is broken.

A hundred horses are prancing.
Their riders are dead.

Guitar solo

Ay, Gypsy Petenera!
Ay, ay, Petenera!

At your burial there were no
good girls.
Girls who give the dead Christ
their locks of hair
and wear white mantillas
to the fair.

Those who buried you
were sinister folk.
Folk with their hearts
in their heads,
who followed you, weeping,
through the back alleys.

Ay, Gypsy Petenera!
Ay, ay, Petenera!

DE PROFUNDIS

The hundred lovers
sleep forever
beneath the dry earth.
Andalusia,
long red roads.
Cordova,
green olive trees
to hang a hundred crosses
in their memory.
The hundred lovers
sleep eternally.

Knell

In the yellow towers
toll the bells.

On the yellow winds
the bell tones bloom.

Down the road
Death goes crowned
with wilted orange blossoms.
She sings and sings
a song
on her white guitar,
sings and sings and sings.

In the yellow towers
the bells stop ringing.

The wind in the dust
is a ship's silver prow.

Two Girls

for Máximo Quijano

La Lola

Under the orange tree
she washes sheets of cotton.
She has green eyes
and a violet voice.

Ay, love
beneath the orange in blossom!

The water in the canal
ran full of sun.
In the little olive grove
a sparrow sang.

Ay, love
beneath the orange in blossom!

When La Lola
has used up all her soap,
the young bullfighters will come.

Ay, love
beneath the orange in blossom!

Amparo

Amparo,
how alone you are in your house,
all dressed in white!

(The line between jasmine
and spikenard.)

You hear the marvelous
fountains of your courtyard,
and the fragile yellow trill
of the canary.

In the afternoon you see
the cypresses tremble with birds
while you slowly embroider
letters upon the canvas.

Amparo,
how alone you are in your house,
all dressed in white!

Amparo,
it's so hard to tell you
I love you!

Flamenco Vignettes

for Manuel Torres, "Niño de Jerez," descended from Pharaohs

Portrait of Silverio Franconeti

Between Italian
and flamenco,
how did
that Silverio sing?

Thick honey of Italy
mixed with Spanish lemon
ran in the deep lament
of the *siguiriya* singer.

His cry was terrifying.
The old ones say
it made one's hair stand on end,
and cracked the quicksilver
of the mirrors.

He moved through the chords
without breaking them.
He was a creator
and a gardener,
builder of arbors
of silence.

Now his melody
sleeps amid the echoes.
Pure and definitive
to the last reverberation!

JUAN BREVA

Juan Breva
body of a giant
voice of a little girl.

There was nothing like his quaver.
It was pain itself
singing behind a smile.

He evokes the lemon groves
of a sleeping Málaga.
In his wail, a taste
of sea salt.

Like Homer, he sang blind.
His voice had something
of a sunless sea
and an orange squeezed dry.

Café Singer

Lamps of crystal
and green mirrors.

Upon the dark stage
La Parrala carries on
a conversation
with death.
The flame
does not come,
and she calls it again.
The people
breathe sobs.
In the green mirrors
long trains of silk
begin to move.

Death Lament

for Miguel Benítez

*In the black sky
yellow serpents.*

I came into this world with eyes
and I leave without them.
God of the greatest sorrow!

And then
an oil lamp and a blanket
on the ground.

I wanted to go
where the good people go.
And I have arrived. My God!...
But then
an oil lamp and a blanket
on the ground.

Little yellow lemon,
lemon tree.
Throw your little lemons
to the wind.
Now you know! Because then,
then,
an oil lamp and a blanket
on the ground.

In the black sky
yellow serpents.

Conjure

The twitching hand
like a Medusa
blinds the oil lamp's
aching eye.

Ace of clubs.
Cross of scissors.

Above the white smoke
of the incense, it seems
a bit like a mole,
an uncertain butterfly.

Ace of clubs.
Cross of scissors.

It clutches a heart
invisible. Can you see it?
A heart
reflected on the wind.

Ace of clubs.
Cross of scissors.

Memento

When I die
bury me with my guitar
beneath the sand.

When I die
among the oranges
and the mint.

When I die
bury me, if you like
in a weather vane.

When I die!

Three Cities

for Pilar Zubiaurre

Malagueña

Death
enters and leaves
the tavern.

Black horses
and sinister people pass
down the deep roads
of the guitar.

There's a smell of salt
and female blood
in the fevered spikenards
of the seashore.

Death
enters and leaves
leaves and enters
the tavern.

Neighborhood of Cordova
Nocturnal Theme

In the house they defend themselves
against the stars.
The night crumbles.
Inside, a dead girl
with a rose of flesh
hidden in her hair.
Six nightingales mourn her
at the window bars.

People pass, sighing
with open guitars.

Dance

La Carmen is dancing
through the streets of Seville
with white hair
and shining eyes.

Girls,
close the curtains!

Around her head
a yellow serpent coils
and she dreams as she dances
of lovers of days gone by.

Girls,
close the curtains!

The streets are empty.
In their depths, one can sense
the hearts of Andalusia
looking for their old thorns.

Girls,
close the curtains!

Six Caprices

for Regino Sainz de la Maza

Riddle of the guitar

At the round
crossroads
six maidens
dance.
Three of flesh
and three of silver.
Yesterday's dreams seek them out,
but a golden Polyphemus
holds them in his embrace.
The guitar!

Oil Lamp

Oh, how gravely
the lamp's flame meditates!

Like an Indian fakir
it gazes at its golden entrails
and eclipses itself
dreaming of windless atmospheres.

Incandescent stork
it pecks from its nest
at the massive shadows
and glances, trembling
at the round eyes
of the dead Gypsy boy.

CASTANET

Castanet.
Castanet.
Castanet.
Sonorous scarab.

In the spider
of the hand
you curl
the warm air
and drown
in your wooden trilling.

Castanet.
Castanet.
Castanet.
Sonorous scarab.

Prickly Pear

Savage Laocoön.

How good you look
beneath the half moon!

Player with multiple balls.

How good you are
at menacing the wind!

Daphne and Attis
know your pain.
Inexplicable.

Agave

Petrified octopus.

You cinch ashen straps
around the belly of the mountain
and fill its passes
with impressive teeth.

Petrified octopus.

Cross

The cross.
(The end point
of the road.)

Sees itself in the canal.
(Points of suspense....)

Scene of the Lieutenant Colonel of the Civil Guard

Flag room

Lt. Colonel: I am the Lieutenant Colonel of the Civil Guard.

Sergeant: Yes, sir.

LC: And no one can contradict me.

S: No, sir.

LC: I have three stars and twenty crosses.

S: Yes, sir.

LC: The Cardinal Archbishop of Toledo, with his twenty-four purple tassels, saluted me.

S: Yes, sir.

LC: I am the Lieutenant. I am the Lieutenant. I am the Lieutenant Colonel of the Civil Guard!

(Romeo and Juliet, celestial, white and gold, embrace on the tobacco garden of the cigar box. The Colonel caresses the barrel of a gun, full of submarine shadows. A voice outside.)

Moon, moon, moon, moon,
of the olive season.
Cazorla shows her tower
and Benamejí conceals it.

Moon, moon, moon, moon.
A rooster crows on the moon.
Mr. Mayor, your little girls
are gazing at the moon.

LC: What's going on?

S: A Gypsy.

(The Gypsy boy's gaze, like a young mule's, darkens and enlarges the irises of the Lieutenant Colonel of the Civil Guard.)

LC: I am the Lieutenant Colonel of the Civil Guard.

S: Yes, sir.

LC: And you, who are you?

Gypsy: A Gypsy.

LC: And what is a Gypsy?

G: Could be anything.

LC: What is your name?

G: You said it.

LC: What did you say?

G: Gypsy.

S: I found him and brought him here.

LC: Where were you?

G: On the bridge of the rivers.

LC: But, what rivers?

G: All rivers.

LC: And what were you doing there?

G: Building a cinnamon tower.

LC: Sergeant!

S: At your command, Lieutenant Colonel of the Civil Guard.

G: I have invented wings to fly, and flown. Brimstone and roses are on my lips.

LC: Ay!

G: Although I don't need wings, for I can fly without them. Clouds and rings in my blood.

LC: Ayyy!

G: In January I have lemon blossoms.

LC: Ayyyyy! *(Writhing)*

G: And oranges in the snow.

LC: Ayyyy, boom, bim, bam! *(He falls dead.)*

(The tobacco-and-coffee soul of the Lieutenant Colonel of the Civil Guard flies out the window.)

Sergeant: Help!

(In the patio of the barracks, four Civil Guards beat the Gypsy.)

Song of the Beaten Gypsy

Twenty-four blows.
Twenty-five blows.
Afterwards, by night, my mother
will wrap me in silver foil.

Civil Guards of the highway,
give me a few sips of water.
Water with fish and with ships.
Water, water, water, water.

Ay, Commander of the Civil Guards
upstairs in your office!
There will be no handkerchiefs of silk
for me to wipe my face with!

July 5, 1925

Dialogue of Amargo

Countryside

A voice:

Amargo.
The oleanders of my patio.
Heart of bitter almond.
Amargo.

(Three young men with wide hats appear.)

First young man: We're going to get there late.
Second young man: Night throws itself over us.
1st: And him?
2nd: He's coming behind.
1st: *(In a loud voice)* Amargo!
Amargo: *(From afar)* I'm coming!
2nd: *(Shouting)* Amargo!
Amargo: *(Calmly)* I'm coming!

(Pause)

1st: What beautiful olive groves!
2nd: Yes, they are.

(Long silence.)

1st: I don't like to travel at night.
2nd: Me neither.
1st: Night was made for sleeping.
2nd: That's right.

(Frogs and crickets raise the arch of an Andalusian summer.
Amargo walks with his hands in his belt.)

Amargo:

Ay yayayay!
I asked death a question.
Ay yayayay!

(The cry of his song puts a circumflex accent, both acute and grave, on the hearts of those who've heard it.)

1st: *(From far away)* Amargo!
2nd: *(Almost lost)* Amargooo!

(Silence)

(Amargo is alone in the middle of the road. He half closes his big green eyes and tightens his cloth jacket around his body. High mountains surround him. His large silver watch ticks quietly in his pocket at each step.)

(A horseman comes galloping down the highway.)

Horseman: *(Halting the horse)* Good evening!
Amargo: The peace of God.
H: Are you going to Granada?
A: I am going to Granada.
H: Then let's go together.
A: Sounds good.
H: Why not mount behind me on the horse?
A: Because my feet aren't hurting.
H: I come from Malaga.
A: Alright.
H: My brothers are there.
A: *(Annoyed)* How many?
H: Three. They sell knives. That's their business.
A: May it keep them well.
H: Of silver and gold.
A: A knife is just a knife.
H: That's where you're wrong.
A: Oh?
H: Knives of gold go straight to the heart. Those of silver cut the neck like a blade of grass.
A: They don't cut bread?
H: Men break bread with their hands.
A: That's true.

(The horse gets restless.)

H: Whoa, there!
A: It's the night.

(The undulating road bends the animal's shadow.)

H: Do you want a knife?
A: No.
H: Look, I'm giving it to you.
A: But I'm not taking it.
H: You won't have another chance.
A: Who knows?
H: Other knives are no good. Other knives are timid and shocked by blood. Those we sell are cold. Understand? They go in, seeking the warmest place, and there they stop.

(Amargo is silent. His right hand grows cold, as if it were grasping a bar of gold.)

H: What a beautiful knife!

(He draws out a knife of gold. Its point gleams like a candle's flame.)

A: Is it worth a lot?
H: Come on, don't you want this one?
A: I already said no.
H: Boy, mount up with me!
A: I'm not tired yet.

(The horse takes fright again.)

H: *(Jerking the reins.)* What a horse!
A: It's the darkness.

(Pause)

H: As I was saying, my three brothers are in Malaga. They sell so many knives! The Cathedral alone bought two thousand, to adorn all the altars and make a crown for the tower. Many ships inscribe their names on them. On the shore, humble fishermen light themselves by night with the gleam that their sharp blades give off.
A: It's a beauty!
H: Who can deny it?

(The night grows heavy as a hundred-year wine. The fat serpent of the South opens its eyes in the early morning, and sleepers feel an infinite desire to throw themselves off the balcony, to the strange, perverse magic of perfume and distance.)

A: Seems like we've lost our way.
H: *(Stopping the horse.)* Oh?
A: While we were talking.
H: Aren't those the lights of Granada?
A: I don't know.
H: The world is very big.

A: As though no one lived there.
H: You said it.
A: It makes me feel hopeless! Ay yayayay!
H: Because that's where you're going. And what are you doing?
A: What am I doing?
H: Once you are in your place, what do you intend to do?
A: To do?
H: I ride this horse and sell knives. But if I didn't, what would happen?
A: What would happen?

(Pause.)

H: We're coming to Granada.
A: Is it possible?
H: Look how the lights shine on the balconies.
A: Yes, I see.
H: Now you will not refuse to ride with me.
A: Wait a little….
H: Let's go—get up! Get up quick. We must arrive before dawn.
And take this knife—my gift to you!
A: Ay yayayay!

(The horseman helps Amargo mount. They head down the road to Granada.
The deep mountains are covered with hemlocks and nettles.)

Song of Amargo's Mother

They bring him here on my bed sheet
on my oleanders and my palm.

On the twenty-seventh day of August
with a little gold knife.

The cross. But we keep on going!
He was brown and bitter.

Neighbors, give me a pitcher
of brass with lemonade.

The cross. Let no one cry.
Amargo is there on the moon.

July 9, 1925

Selected Readings

Primary Sources

García Lorca, Federico. *Obras Completas*, edited by Arturo del Hoyo, Madrid: Aguilar, 1986
_____. *Poema del Cante Jondo; Romancero Gitano: Conferencias y Poemas*. Stockcero, 2010. Includes related speeches and discussions by the poet.

Secondary Sources

Translations

García Lorca, Federico. *Federico García Lorca: Collected Poems*, edited by Christopher Maurer, revised edition; Farrar, Straus and Giroux, 2002.
_____. *Poem of the Deep Song*. Translated by Ralph Angel, Sarabande Books, 2006.

Biography

Gibson, Ian. *Federico García Lorca, a Life*. Pantheon Books, 1989.
Stainton, Leslie. *Lorca, a Dream of Life*. Farrar, Straus and Giroux, 1999.
Roberts, Stephan. *Deep Song: The Life and Work of Federico García Lorca*. Reaktion Books, 2020.

Criticism

Newton, Candelas. *Understanding Federico García Lorca*. University of South Carolina Press, 1995
Stone, Rob. *The Flamenco Tradition in the Works of Federico García Lorca and Carlos Saura*. Lewiston: E. Mellen Press, 2004.
Bonaddio, Federico. *A Companion to Federico García Lorca*. Woodbridge, UK : Tamesis ; Rochester, New York: Boydell & Brewer, 2007.

www.ingramcontent.com/pod-product-compliance
Lightning Source LLC
Chambersburg PA
CBHW031711230426
43668CB00006B/183